Ԛ

last-minute meals

THE AUSTRALIAN
Women's Weekly

CONTENTS

Australian cup and spoon measurements are metric. A conversion chart appears on page 77.

This book could be subtitled "Out of the frying pan and onto the table", so quick and simple to prepare are its contents. With tasty, honest food like this – food that doesn't require pre-planning or do-ahead steps – you'll never be caught off-guard if unexpected guests show up, or tempted into takeaway if you're late home from work.

Pamela Clark

Food Director

CHICKEN AND BROCCOLI
WITH OYSTER SAUCE

on the table in 20 minutes serves 4
nutritional count per serving 12.7g total fat (2.9g
saturated fat); 1179kJ (282 cal); 8.1g carbohydrate;
31.7g protein; 3.8g fibre

½ cup (125ml) chicken stock
¼ cup (60ml) oyster sauce
2 teaspoons cornflour
2 teaspoons caster sugar
½ teaspoon sesame oil
1 tablespoon vegetable oil
500g chicken breast fillets, sliced thinly
4 green onions, chopped
1 tablespoon grated ginger
2 teaspoons crushed garlic
500g broccoli florets
2 tablespoons water

1 Whisk stock, sauce, cornflour, sugar and
sesame oil in small bowl until well combined.
2 Heat half of the vegetable oil in wok pan;
stir-fry chicken, in batches, until just cooked
through.
3 Heat remaining vegetable oil in same wok;
stir-fry onion, ginger, garlic, broccoli and the
water until broccoli is tender. Return chicken to
wok with sauce mixture; stir-fry until chicken is
hot and sauce boils and thickens slightly.

CHICKEN

coriander and chilli grilled chicken

1 Make coriander chilli sauce.
2 Cook chicken, in batches, on heated oiled grill plate (or grill or barbecue) until almost cooked through. Brush about two-thirds of the coriander chilli sauce all over chicken; cook 5 minutes or until chicken is cooked through.
3 Meanwhile, make chickpea salad.
4 Serve chicken, topped with remaining sauce, with chickpea salad.
coriander chilli sauce Blend or process onion, garlic, chilli, coriander and sugar until finely chopped. Add fish sauce and juice; blend until well combined.
chickpea salad Place ingredients in large bowl; toss gently to combine.

CHICKEN PHO

on the table in 20 minutes serves 4
nutritional count per serving 10.6g total fat (3.3g saturated fat); 1154kJ (276 cal); 9.9g carbohydrate; 34.5g protein; 1.7g fibre

1.5 litres (6 cups) chicken stock
2 teaspoons grated ginger
1 teaspoon crushed garlic
¼ cup (60ml) fish sauce
1 tablespoon chopped lemon grass
1 teaspoon sambal oelek
4 green onions, sliced thinly
100g dried rice noodles
4 cups (400g) shredded cooked chicken
1 cup (80g) bean sprouts
½ cup firmly packed fresh mint leaves
¼ cup firmly packed fresh coriander leaves

1 Bring stock, ginger, garlic, sauce and lemon grass to the boil in large saucepan. Reduce heat; simmer, covered, 8 minutes. Remove from heat; stir in sambal oelek and onion.
2 Meanwhile, place noodles in medium heatproof bowl; cover with boiling water. Stand until just tender; drain.
3 Divide noodles among serving bowls; top with chicken. Ladle soup over chicken; top with sprouts, mint and coriander.

note You need to purchase a large barbecued chicken weighing about 900g for this recipe.

CORIANDER AND CHILLI GRILLED CHICKEN

on the table in 25 minutes serves 4
nutritional count per serving 18.7g total fat (4.6g saturated fat); 1664kJ (398 cal); 16.7g carbohydrate; 38.2g protein; 5.7g fibre

6 chicken thigh fillets (660g), halved
coriander chilli sauce
8 green onions, chopped coarsely
2 teaspoons crushed garlic
1 teaspoon chopped red chilli
¼ cup loosely packed fresh coriander
1 teaspoon sugar
1 tablespoon fish sauce
¼ cup (60ml) lime juice
chickpea salad
2 x 300g cans chickpeas, rinsed, drained
2 medium egg tomatoes (150g),
    chopped coarsely
2 green onions, chopped finely
2 tablespoons lime juice
1 cup chopped fresh coriander
1 tablespoon olive oil

chicken pho

CHICKEN AND CORN
on the table in **1 hour (+ cooling)** makes **24**

Boil, steam or microwave 24 baby new potatoes until just tender; drain. Cool. Cut shallow slice from top of each potato. Using a melon-baller, carefully scoop out about two-thirds of the flesh of each potato into a medium bowl; stir in 1½ cups finely chopped barbecue chicken, 125g canned creamed corn, 2 tablespoons sour cream, 3 finely chopped green onions and ¼ cup finely grated parmesan cheese until combined. Divide filling into potato shells, place on oiled oven tray. Bake at 200°C/180°C fan-forced about 15 minutes or until heated through.

CHORIZO
on the table in **50 minutes** serves **4**

Boil, steam or microwave 8 coliban potatoes until tender; drain. Heat 1 teaspoon olive oil in small frying pan; cook 70g finely chopped chorizo sausage, stirring, 3 minutes or until crisp. Drain. Cook 1 clove crushed garlic in same pan, stirring over low heat, until just fragrant. Return chorizo to pan with 1 cup canned crushed tomatoes; simmer, uncovered, until mixture reduces by half. Cut shallow slice from top of each potato; using teaspoon, scoop flesh from each top into medium bowl, discard skin. Scoop about two-thirds of the flesh from each potato into same bowl; reserve potato shells. Mash potato until smooth; stir in chorizo mixture and ⅓ cup sour cream. Place potato shells on oiled oven tray; divide filling into shells, sprinkle with 2 tablespoons pizza cheese. Bake at 200°C/180°C fan-forced 15 minutes or until heated through.

BAKED POTATOES

PEA PUREE

on the table in **1 hour (+ cooling)** makes **24**

Boil, steam or microwave 24 baby new potatoes
until just tender; drain. Cool. Boil, steam or
microwave 1⅔ cups frozen peas until just
tender; drain. Cut shallow slice from top of each
potato. Using a melon-baller, carefully scoop
out about two-thirds of the flesh of each potato;
reserve flesh. Blend or process peas with
reserved potato flesh and 40g chopped butter
until pureed; stir in ¼ cup finely grated parmesan
cheese until combined. Divide filling into potato
shells and sprinkle with extra finely grated
parmesan cheese. Place potatoes on oiled oven
tray. Bake in 200°C/180°C fan-forced oven
about 15 minutes or until heated through.

CREAMED CORN

on the table in **50 minutes** serves **4**

Boil, steam or microwave 8 coliban potatoes
until tender; drain. Heat 1 teaspoon vegetable oil
in small frying pan; cook 30g coarsely chopped
prosciutto slices, stirring, 2 minutes or until crisp.
Cut shallow slice from top of each potato; using
teaspoon, scoop flesh from each top into
medium bowl, discard skin. Scoop about two-
thirds of the flesh from each potato into same
bowl; reserve potato shells. Mash potato until
smooth; stir in prosciutto, 125g canned creamed
corn and 2 tablespoons finely chopped fresh
coriander. Place potato shells on oiled oven tray;
divide filling into shells. Bake at 200°C/180°C fan-
forced 15 minutes or until heated through.

thai-style pumpkin and chicken soup

CHICKEN SANG CHOY BOW

on the table in **15 minutes** serves **4**
nutritional count per serving 26.2g total fat (7.2g
saturated fat); 2207kJ (528 cal); 17.4g carbohydrate;
53.2g protein; 3.7g fibre

1 tablespoon peanut oil
1kg chicken mince
2 teaspoons crushed garlic
230g can bamboo shoots, drained,
    chopped finely
1 teaspoon chopped chilli
1 stalk celery (150g), trimmed,
    chopped finely
1 medium red capsicum (200g),
    chopped finely
2 tablespoons soy sauce
1 tablespoon rice vinegar
1½ tablespoons lime juice
2 teaspoons cornflour
½ cup (125ml) chicken stock
100g packet fried noodles
¼ cup chopped fresh coriander
8 iceberg lettuce leaves, trimmed

1 Heat oil in large frying pan; cook chicken
and garlic over high heat, stirring, until chicken
changes colour.
2 Stir in bamboo shoots, chilli, celery, capsicum,
sauce, vinegar, juice and combined cornflour
and stock; bring to the boil. Reduce heat;
simmer, uncovered, until sauce thickens.
3 Just before serving, stir in noodles and
coriander.
4 Serve chicken mixture in lettuce cups.
serve with **extra soy sauce for dipping.**

THAI-STYLE PUMPKIN
AND CHICKEN SOUP

on the table in **15 minutes** serves **4**
nutritional count per serving 55.6g total fat (39.9g
saturated fat); 2943kJ (704 cal); 20.8g carbohydrate;
28.2g protein; 8.6g

¼ cup (60g) red curry paste
2 x 510g cans pumpkin soup
2 x 400ml cans coconut milk
1 cup (250ml) chicken stock
2 chicken breast fillets (340g), sliced thinly
4 green onions, sliced thinly
2 tablespoons chopped fresh coriander

1 Cook curry paste, stirring, in heated oiled
medium saucepan until fragrant.
2 Add pumpkin soup, coconut milk and stock
to pan; bring to the boil. Add chicken and stir
until cooked through.
3 Just before serving, stir in onion and coriander.

chicken sang choy bow

chicken satay

CHICKEN SATAY

on the table in 15 minutes serves 4
nutritional count per serving 35.3g total fat (15g
saturated fat); 2458kJ (588 cal); 18.6g carbohydrate;
48g protein; 3.4g fibre

1 tablespoon peanut oil
800g chicken tenderloins, halved
2 large brown onions (400g), sliced thickly
1 teaspoon crushed garlic
¼ cup (60ml) chicken stock
⅔ cup (160ml) coconut milk
¾ cup (180ml) satay sauce

1 Heat oil in wok or large frying pan; stir-fry
chicken, in batches, until browned all over and
cooked through.
2 Place onion and garlic in same wok; stir-fry
until onion softens.
3 Return chicken to wok with remaining
ingredients; stir-fry until sauce thickens slightly.
serve with **green onion curls.**

tip The spiciness of this dish will depend on the brand
of satay sauce you use.

chicken tikka

CHICKEN TIKKA

on the table in 20 minutes serves 4
nutritional count per serving 22.5g total fat (6.4g
saturated fat); 1822kJ (436 cal); 8.5g carbohydrate;
49.3g protein; 1.5g fibre

2 tablespoons tikka masala paste
2 tablespoons mango chutney
1kg chicken thigh fillets, sliced thinly
⅓ cup (80ml) chicken stock
½ cup (140g) yogurt
½ cup chopped fresh coriander
2 teaspoons lime juice
1 fresh red thai chilli, sliced thinly

1 Combine paste, chutney and chicken in
large bowl.
2 Heat wok; stir-fry chicken mixture, in batches,
until chicken is browned all over.
3 Return chicken to wok, add remaining
ingredients; bring to the boil. Reduce heat;
simmer, uncovered, about 5 minutes or until
chicken is cooked through.
serve with **steamed basmati rice; top with a drizzle of
yogurt and fresh coriander leaves.**

WOK-TOSSED HONEY SOY CHICKEN WINGS

on the table in 25 minutes serves 4
nutritional count per serving 43.1g total fat (11.5g saturated fat); 2905kJ (695 cal); 19.1g carbohydrate; 59g protein; 0.4g fibre

12 large chicken wings (1.5kg)
2 teaspoons crushed garlic
1 tablespoon grated ginger
1 tablespoon peanut oil
1 tablespoon fish sauce
1 tablespoon soy sauce
¼ cup (90g) honey
2 green onions, sliced thinly

1 Cut wing tips from chicken; cut wings in half at joint. Combine chicken, garlic and ginger in large bowl.
2 Heat oil in wok; stir-fry chicken mixture, in batches, until chicken is browned.
3 Return chicken mixture to wok. Add sauces and honey; stir-fry until well coated. Cover wok; cook, stirring occasionally, about 10 minutes or until chicken is cooked through. Serve topped with onion.

pesto chicken salad

PESTO CHICKEN SALAD

on the table in 25 minutes serves 4
nutritional count per serving 23.2g total fat (5.5g saturated fat); 1622kJ (388 cal); 3.1g carbohydrate; 40.5g protein; 2.3g fibre

⅓ cup (90g) basil pesto
2 tablespoons balsamic vinegar
4 chicken breast fillets (680g)
6 medium egg tomatoes (450g), halved
125g baby rocket leaves
1 tablespoon olive oil

1 Combine pesto and vinegar in small bowl; divide mixture in two portions.
2 Place chicken and tomato on oven tray; brush one portion of the pesto mixture over chicken and tomato.
3 Cook tomato on heated oiled grill plate (or grill or barbecue) until just softened; remove from plate. Cook chicken on same grill plate until browned both sides and cooked through. Stand 5 minutes; slice thickly.
4 Place tomato and chicken in large bowl with rocket, oil and remaining pesto mixture; toss gently to combine.

wok-tossed honey soy chicken wings

mustard and rosemary chicken

MUSTARD AND
ROSEMARY CHICKEN

on the table in 20 minutes serves 4
nutritional count per serving 18.6g total fat (6.2g
saturated fat); 1818kJ (435 cal); 21.1g carbohydrate;
42g protein; 5.5g fibre

4 single chicken breast fillets (680g)
1 tablespoon wholegrain mustard
1 tablespoon lemon juice
1 tablespoon olive oil
1 tablespoon chopped fresh rosemary
1 teaspoon crushed garlic
600g baby new potatoes, quartered
250g baby spinach leaves
20g butter
1 medium lemon (140g), quartered

1 Combine chicken, mustard, juice, oil,
rosemary and garlic in medium bowl.
2 Cook chicken, in batches, on heated oiled
grill plate (or grill or barbecue) until chicken is
browned both sides and cooked through.
3 Meanwhile, boil, steam or microwave
potatoes until just tender; drain. Place hot
potatoes in large bowl with spinach and butter;
toss gently until butter melts and spinach
just wilts.
4 Serve chicken with vegetables and lemon
quarters.

note You need two lemons for this recipe.

chicken and sweet soy stir-fry

CHICKEN AND SWEET SOY STIR-FRY

on the table in 15 minutes serves 4
nutritional count per serving 17.5g total fat (4.4g
saturated fat); 2550kJ (610 cal); 61.7g carbohydrate;
48.4g protein; 4g fibre

450g hokkien noodles
1 tablespoon peanut oil
3 cups (510g) coarsely chopped cooked
    chicken
6 green onions, sliced
1 teaspoon crushed garlic
2 cups (160g) bean sprouts
½ cup (125ml) chicken stock
2 tablespoons sweet chilli sauce
¼ cup (60ml) kecap manis

1 Place noodles in small heatproof bowl; cover
with boiling water, separate with fork, drain.
2 Heat oil in wok; cook chicken, onion and
garlic until chicken is heated through.
3 Add noodles, sprouts and combined stock,
sauce and kecap manis; stir-fry until noodles are
heated through.

note You need to purchase a large barbecued chicken
weighing about 900g for this recipe.

chicken laksa

CHICKEN LAKSA

on the table in **15 minutes** serves **4**
nutritional count per serving 61.5g total fat (41.3g saturated fat); 4539kJ (1086 cal); 74.5g carbohydrate; 55.4g protein; 8.7g fibre

450g fresh egg noodles
1 teaspoon peanut oil
¼ cup (75g) laksa paste
3¼ cups (810ml) coconut milk
1 litre (4 cups) chicken stock
2 tablespoons lime juice
1 tablespoon sugar
1 tablespoon fish sauce
6 kaffir lime leaves, torn
3 cups (510g) coarsely chopped
    cooked chicken
1 cup (80g) bean sprouts
½ cup loosely packed fresh mint leaves

1 Rinse noodles in strainer under hot running water. Separate noodles with fork; drain.
2 Heat oil in large saucepan; cook paste, stirring, until fragrant. Stir in coconut milk, stock, juice, sugar, sauce and lime leaves; bring to the boil. Reduce heat; simmer, covered, 3 minutes. Add chicken; stir until laksa is heated through.
3 Divide noodles among serving bowls. Ladle laksa over noodles; top with sprouts and mint.

note You need to purchase a large barbecued chicken weighing about 900g for this recipe.

CHICKEN, BASIL AND WOMBOK SALAD

on the table in **15 minutes** serves **4**
nutritional count per serving 24g total fat (5.4g saturated fat); 1693kJ (405 cal); 7.6g carbohydrate; 38.1g protein; 3.4g fibre

1 teaspoon crushed garlic
¼ cup (60ml) peanut oil
¼ cup (60ml) lime juice
2 tablespoons fish sauce
1 tablespoon sugar
3 cups (510g) shredded cooked chicken
4 cups (320g) finely shredded wombok
4 green onions, sliced thinly
¼ cup chopped fresh basil

1 Place garlic, oil, juice, sauce and sugar in screw-top jar; shake well.
2 Place chicken, wombok, onion and basil in large bowl with dressing; toss gently to combine.

note You need to purchase a medium wombok, as well as a large barbecued chicken weighing about 900g for this recipe.

creamy red pesto chicken with gnocchi

CREAMY RED PESTO CHICKEN WITH GNOCCHI

on the table in 20 minutes serves 4
nutritional count per serving 66g total fat (29.9g saturated fat); 4372kJ (1046 cal); 38.9g carbohydrate; 68.7g protein; 3.3g fibre

1 tablespoon olive oil
8 chicken thigh cutlets (1.3kg)
500g fresh gnocchi
1 teaspoon crushed garlic
½ cup (125ml) dry white wine
¼ cup (60g) sun-dried tomato pesto
300ml cream
¼ cup loosely packed small fresh basil leaves

1 Heat oil in large frying pan; cook chicken, covered, until browned on both sides and cooked through.
2 Meanwhile, cook gnocchi in large saucepan of boiling water, uncovered, until tender; drain.
3 Remove chicken from pan; cover to keep warm. Drain fat from pan. Add garlic to pan; cook until fragrant. Add wine; simmer, uncovered, until most of the liquid has evaporated. Stir in pesto and cream; bring to the boil.
4 Serve chicken with gnocchi and sauce, sprinkled with basil.

note Fresh gnocchi is available from the refrigerated section in most supermarkets.

tandoori chicken salad

TANDOORI CHICKEN SALAD

on the table in 15 minutes serves 4
nutritional count per serving 15.1g total fat (4.7g saturated fat); 1605kJ (384 cal); 11.6g carbohydrate; 47g protein; 3.7g fibre

½ cup (140g) yogurt
1½ tablespoons tandoori paste
750g chicken tenderloins
¾ cup (200g) yogurt, extra
¼ cup (60ml) mint sauce
250g mesclun
4 large egg tomatoes (360g), chopped
2 lebanese cucumbers (260g), chopped

1 Combine yogurt, paste and chicken in large bowl.
2 Cook chicken mixture, in batches, on heated oiled grill plate (or grill or barbecue) until browned on both sides and cooked through.
3 Meanwhile, combine extra yogurt and sauce in small bowl.
4 Divide mesclun among serving plates, top with tomato, cucumber and chicken. Serve drizzled with yogurt mint sauce.

VEAL MARSALA

on the table in 20 minutes serves 4
nutritional count per serving 12.5g total fat (2.2g
saturated fat); 1229kJ (294 cal); 9.2g carbohydrate;
30.2g protein; 2.1g fibre

2 tablespoons olive oil
4 veal leg steaks (500g)
1 medium brown onion (150g), chopped finely
250g button mushrooms, sliced thinly
¼ cup (60ml) marsala
⅔ cup (160ml) beef stock
1 tablespoon chopped fresh chives

1 Heat oil in large frying pan; cook veal until
browned on both sides and cooked as desired.
Remove from pan.
2 Add onion to same pan; cook, stirring, until soft.
3 Add mushrooms to pan with marsala and
stock; stir over heat until mixture boils and
thickens slightly.
4 Serve marsala sauce over sliced veal; sprinkle
with chives.
serve with soft polenta.

BEEF
& VEAL

beef with mushroom and red wine sauce

BEEF KOFTA WITH HUMMUS

on the table in **30 minutes** serves 4
nutritional count per serving 17g total fat (6.3g saturated fat); 1513kJ (362 cal); 16.8g carbohydrate; 33.2g protein; 4.9g fibre

500g beef mince
1 cup (70g) stale breadcrumbs
2 teaspoons finely grated lemon rind
1 teaspoon ground cumin
1 teaspoon ground coriander
1 teaspoon crushed garlic
1 egg, beaten lightly
2 medium tomatoes (380g), chopped coarsely
1 tablespoon chopped fresh flat-leaf parsley
½ cup (125g) hummus
pinch paprika

1 Combine beef, breadcrumbs, rind, cumin, coriander, garlic and egg in medium bowl. Divide mixture into 12 portions; roll each portion into a sausage shape, then thread onto 12 skewers.
2 Cook kofta in batches, on heated oiled grill plate (or grill or barbecue) until cooked through.
3 Meanwhile, combine tomato and parsley in medium bowl.
4 Serve kofta with hummus, sprinkled with paprika, and tomato mixture.
serve with **pitta bread.**

BEEF WITH MUSHROOM AND RED WINE SAUCE

on the table in **30 minutes** serves 4
nutritional count per serving 20.8g total fat (8.9g saturated fat); 1735kJ (415 cal); 2.9g carbohydrate; 47g protein; 3.6g fibre

1 tablespoon olive oil
4 beef rib-eye steaks (800g)
30g butter
8 spring onions (200g), quartered
1 teaspoon crushed garlic
1 cup (250ml) dry red wine
½ cup (125ml) beef stock
6 flat mushrooms, quartered
2 tablespoons chopped fresh flat-leaf parsley

1 Heat oil in large frying pan; cook beef until browned on both sides and cooked as desired. Remove from pan.
2 Add butter and onion to same pan; cook, stirring, until onion is browned lightly.
3 Stir in garlic, wine and stock; bring to the boil. Reduce heat; simmer, covered, 10 minutes.
4 Add mushrooms; cook, stirring, until mushrooms are soft. Stir in parsley.
5 Serve beef with sauce.
serve with **kumara mash.**

beef kofta with hummus

lemon pepper veal cutlets

SAUSAGES WITH LENTIL AND VEGETABLE SAUCE

on the table in 15 minutes serves 4
nutritional count per serving 57.8g total fat (25.4g saturated fat); 3164kJ (757 cal); 17g carbohydrate; 38.6g protein; 10.4g fibre

8 thick beef sausages
1 tablespoon olive oil
1 medium brown onion (150g),
    chopped finely
1 teaspoon crushed garlic
2 stalks celery (300g), trimmed,
    chopped finely
3 bacon rashers (210g), chopped
2 medium zucchini (240g), sliced
½ cup (125ml) chicken stock
400g can tomatoes
1 teaspoon chopped chilli
1 tablespoon tomato paste
410g can brown lentils, rinsed, drained
2 teaspoons chopped fresh thyme

1 Cook sausages on heated grill plate (or grill or barbecue) until browned all over and cooked through.
2 Meanwhile, heat oil in medium saucepan, add onion and garlic; cook, stirring, until onion softens. Add celery, bacon and zucchini; cook, stirring, until celery softens.
3 Stir in stock, undrained crushed tomatoes, chilli and paste; bring to the boil. Add lentils; stir until heated through.
4 Serve lentil and vegetable sauce with sausages, sprinkled with thyme.

sausages with lentil and vegetable sauce

LEMON PEPPER VEAL CUTLETS

on the table in 15 minutes serves 4
nutritional count per serving 6.2g total fat (2.3g saturated fat); 1058kJ (253 cal); 0.7g carbohydrate; 45.5g protein; 0.2g fibre

8 veal cutlets (1kg)
1 tablespoon lemon pepper seasoning
1 teaspoon crushed garlic
¼ cup (60ml) dry white wine
¾ cup (180ml) chicken stock
1 tablespoon lemon juice
¼ cup chopped fresh chives

1 Sprinkle veal with lemon pepper. Cook veal in heated oiled frying pan until browned on both sides and cooked as desired. Remove from pan; cover to keep warm.
2 Add garlic and wine to same pan; bring to the boil. Add stock and juice; boil, uncovered, until reduced by half. Stir in chives.
3 Serve sauce over veal.
serve with steamed baby potatoes, sour cream and broccolini.

steak and aïoli sandwiches

VEAL STROGANOFF WITH BUTTERED SAGE PASTA

on the table in 20 minutes serves 4
nutritional count per serving 23.4g total fat (11.2g saturated fat); 2487kJ (595 cal); 47.8g carbohydrate; 43.3g protein; 4.3g fibre

250g ricciolini pasta (or other short pasta)
1 tablespoon olive oil
1 small brown onion (80g), sliced thinly
1 teaspoon crushed garlic
2 teaspoons sweet paprika
600g veal steaks, sliced thinly
100g cup mushrooms, sliced thickly
100g button mushrooms, sliced thickly
¼ cup (60ml) red wine
1 tablespoon tomato paste
½ cup (120g) sour cream
½ cup (125ml) beef stock
2 teaspoons cornflour
1 tablespoon chopped fresh sage
30g butter
50g baby spinach leaves

1 Cook pasta in large saucepan of boiling water until just tender.
2 Meanwhile, heat oil in medium saucepan; cook onion, garlic and paprika, stirring, until onion softens. Add veal; cook, stirring, until veal is browned all over.
3 Add mushrooms to pan; cook, stirring, until mushrooms are tender. Add wine; bring to the boil. Stir in paste, cream and combined stock and cornflour; bring to the boil. Reduce heat; simmer, uncovered, until slightly thickened.
4 Drain pasta and return to pan. Stir in sage, butter and spinach; stir until spinach is just wilted. Serve veal stroganoff over pasta mixture.

STEAK AND AIOLI SANDWICHES

on the table in 20 minutes serves 4
nutritional count per serving 21g total fat (5.6g saturated fat); 1864kJ (446 cal); 16.9g carbohydrate; 45.3g protein; 2.9g fibre

8 thin beef fillet steaks (800g)
4 large egg tomatoes (360g), halved
1 tablespoon olive oil
4 slices ciabatta
1 tablespoon shredded fresh basil
1 tablespoon balsamic vinegar
100g mesclun
aïoli
½ cup (75g) mayonnaise
1 teaspoon crushed garlic

1 Cook beef on heated oiled grill plate (or grill or barbecue) until browned on both sides and cooked as desired.
2 Meanwhile, place tomatoes, cut-side up, on tray; drizzle with oil. Grill 10 minutes or until soft.
3 Make aïoli.
4 Toast bread; spread with aïoli, top with steaks and tomatoes, sprinkle with basil and vinegar. Serve with mesclun.
aïoli Combine ingredients in small bowl.

veal stroganoff with buttered sage pasta

veal cutlets with red pesto sauce

VEAL CUTLETS WITH RED PESTO SAUCE

on the table in **15 minutes** serves 4
nutritional count per serving 31g total fat (12.8g saturated fat); 1960kJ (469 cal); 2.1g carbohydrate; 45.1g protein; 1.8g fibre

8 veal cutlets (900g)
1 tablespoon olive oil
200g button mushrooms, sliced
½ cup (125ml) beef stock
⅓ cup (80g) sun-dried tomato pesto
½ cup (125ml) cream
8 fresh basil leaves, torn

1 Cook veal on heated oiled grill plate (or grill or barbecue) until browned on both sides and cooked as desired.
2 Meanwhile, heat oil in medium frying pan; cook mushrooms, stirring, until softened.
3 Add stock, pesto and cream to pan; cook, stirring, until hot, stir in basil.
4 Serve veal with red pesto sauce.
serve with **steamed green beans and whole baby new potatoes.**

steaks with green capsicum salsa

STEAKS WITH GREEN CAPSICUM SALSA

on the table in **15 minutes** serves 4
nutritional count per serving 7.4g total fat (3.2g saturated fat); 907kJ (217 cal); 3.3g carbohydrate; 32.9g protein; 1.2g fibre

4 small beef eye fillet steaks (600g)
green capsicum salsa
2 small green capsicums (300g),
chopped finely
1 small red onion (100g), chopped finely
1 fresh medium red thai chilli, chopped
6 green onions, sliced
¼ cup (60ml) lime juice
2 tablespoons chopped fresh mint

1 Cook beef on heated oiled grill plate (or grill or barbecue) until browned on both sides and cooked as desired.
2 Meanwhile, make green capsicum salsa.
3 Serve beef with salsa.
green capsicum salsa Combine ingredients in medium bowl.
serve with **baby spinach leaves.**

SPICY LAMB NOODLE STIR-FRY

20 minutes   4

21.9g total fat (7g
saturated fat); 2512kJ (601 cal); 50.1g carbohydrate;
48.2g protein; 3.7g fibre

750g lamb strips
1 teaspoon sesame oil
1 tablespoon finely grated orange rind
2 teaspoons crushed garlic
1 teaspoon grated ginger
½ cup (125ml) light soy sauce
1 tablespoon black bean sauce
1 tablespoon brown sugar
250g dried wheat noodles
2 tablespoons peanut oil
200g snow peas, sliced thinly lengthways
1 medium fresh red chilli, sliced
¼ cup (60ml) beef stock

1 Combine lamb with sesame oil, rind, garlic,
ginger, sauces and sugar in large bowl.
2 Cook noodles in large saucepan of boiling
water, uncovered, until just tender; drain.
3 Heat a little of the peanut oil in wok; add snow
peas, stir-fry until tender. Remove from wok.
4 Drain lamb from marinade, reserve marinade.
Heat a little more of the peanut oil in wok;
stir-fry lamb, in batches, until browned and
cooked through.
5 Return snow peas and lamb to wok with
reserved marinade, chilli and stock; bring to the
boil. Add noodles; stir-fry until heated through.

LAMB

lamb cutlets with white bean salad

BUCATINI WITH MOROCCAN LAMB SAUCE

on the table in **30 minutes** serves 4
nutritional count per serving 16.2g total fat (6.3g saturated fat); 2571kJ (615 cal); 73.7g carbohydrate; 38.9g protein; 7.2g fibre

375g bucatini pasta
2 teaspoons olive oil
1 small brown onion (80g), chopped finely
1 teaspoon crushed garlic
500g lamb mince
1 teaspoon ground cumin
½ teaspoon cayenne pepper
½ teaspoon ground cinnamon
2 tablespoons tomato paste
2 x 415g cans tomatoes
1 large zucchini (150g), chopped coarsely
2 tablespoons chopped fresh mint

1 Cook pasta in large saucepan of boiling water until just tender; drain.
2 Meanwhile, heat oil in large saucepan; cook onion and garlic, stirring, until onion is soft. Add lamb; cook, stirring, until lamb changes colour. Add spices; cook, stirring, until fragrant.
3 Stir in tomato paste, undrained crushed tomatoes and zucchini; bring to the boil. Reduce heat; simmer, uncovered, about 15 minutes or until sauce thickens slightly. Stir in mint.
4 Serve pasta topped with sauce.

LAMB CUTLETS WITH WHITE BEAN SALAD

on the table in **15 minutes** serves 4
nutritional count per serving 27.9g total fat (7g saturated fat); 1818kJ (435 cal); 14.1g carbohydrate; 29.3g protein; 6.6g fibre

12 lamb cutlets (900g)
2 x 300g cans white beans, rinsed, drained
3 large egg tomatoes (270g), seeded, chopped finely
2 lebanese cucumbers (260g), seeded, chopped finely
1 small red onion (100g), chopped finely
¼ cup (60ml) lemon juice
1 tablespoon wholegrain mustard
⅓ cup (80ml) olive oil
2 tablespoons chopped fresh flat-leaf parsley

1 Cook lamb, in batches, on heated oiled grill plate (or grill or barbecue) until browned both sides and cooked as desired.
2 Meanwhile, combine white beans with remaining ingredients in medium bowl.
3 Serve cutlets with white bean salad.

bucatini with moroccan lamb sauce

warm lamb, potato and pesto salad

TANDOORI LAMB WITH TOMATO SAMBAL AND MINT RAITA

on the table in **15 minutes** serves **4**
nutritional count per serving 23g total fat (9.8g saturated fat); 2011kJ (481 cal); 31.1g carbohydrate; 34g protein; 4.7g fibre

12 lamb cutlets (900g)
¼ cup (75g) tandoori paste
¾ cup (200g) yogurt
2 medium tomatoes (300g)
1 lebanese cucumber (130g)
1 small red onion (100g)
1 tablespoon lemon juice
1 teaspoon crushed garlic
2 tablespoons fresh mint
2 tablespoons fresh coriander
4 naan bread

1 Combine lamb with paste and ¼ cup of the yogurt in large bowl.
2 Cook lamb mixture, in batches, on heated oiled grill plate (or grill or barbecue) until browned on both sides and cooked as desired.
3 Meanwhile, chop tomatoes, cucumber and onion; combine in medium bowl with juice and garlic.
4 Blend or process remaining yogurt with mint and coriander until smooth (yogurt will become runny).
5 Place naan under preheated grill until warm.
6 Serve cutlets with tomato sambal, mint raita and naan.

tandoori lamb with tomato sambal and mint raita

WARM LAMB, POTATO AND PESTO SALAD

on the table in **15 minutes** serves **4**
nutritional count per serving 23.1g total fat (7.2g saturated fat); 2157kJ (516 cal); 35.9g carbohydrate; 38.3g protein; 5.4g fibre

600g baby new potatoes, chopped
1 tablespoon olive oil
8 lamb fillets (600g)
280g jar char-grilled eggplant,
    drained, chopped
200g baby spinach leaves
8 fresh basil leaves
⅓ cup (80g) char-grilled vegetable pesto
1 tablespoon lemon juice

1 Boil, steam or microwave potatoes until tender; drain.
2 Meanwhile, heat oil in large frying pan; cook lamb until browned all over and cooked as desired. Stand lamb about 2 minutes before slicing thickly.
3 Place warm potato and lamb in large bowl with remaining ingredients; toss gently to combine.

lamb cutlets with beetroot and tzatziki

LEMON AND OLIVE LAMB WITH COUSCOUS

on the table in 20 minutes serves 4
nutritional count per serving 23.6g total fat (10g saturated fat); 2759kJ (660 cal); 44.2g carbohydrate; 62.1g protein; 3.9g fibre

1kg lamb backstrap (eye of loin)
1 cup (250ml) chicken stock
1 cup (200g) couscous
20g butter
2 tablespoons pine nuts
⅓ cup chopped fresh flat-leaf parsley
400g green beans
⅓ cup (80ml) dry white wine
½ cup (125ml) chicken stock, extra
1 tablespoon lemon juice
20g butter, chopped, extra
⅓ cup (50g) black olives

1 Cook lamb in large frying pan until browned all over and cooked as desired. Remove from pan; cover with foil to keep warm.
2 Meanwhile, bring stock to the boil in small saucepan. Place couscous in medium heatproof bowl; pour over hot stock. Stand about 5 minutes, covered, or until liquid is absorbed.
3 Heat butter in small saucepan; cook pine nuts, stirring, until browned lightly. Using a fork, fluff couscous, then stir in pine nuts and parsley.
4 Boil, steam or microwave beans until just tender; drain.
5 Drain excess fat from frying pan. Add wine to pan, bring to the boil. Stir in extra stock and lemon juice; simmer, uncovered, 1 minute or until reduced slightly. Whisk in extra butter, then stir in olives.
6 Serve lamb and sauce with couscous and beans.

LAMB CUTLETS WITH BEETROOT AND TZATZIKI

on the table in 25 minutes serves 4
nutritional count per serving 25.2g total fat (8.2g saturated fat); 1810kJ (433 cal); 17.9g carbohydrate; 30.3g protein; 8.2g fibre

12 lamb cutlets (780g)
2 tablespoons lemon juice
2 cloves garlic, crushed
2 tablespoons olive oil
900g baby beetroot
250g tub tzatziki dip

1 Combine lamb, juice, garlic and oil in large bowl.
2 Trim leaves from beetroot; discard leaves. Boil, steam or microwave unpeeled beetroot until tender, drain; cool. Peel beetroot; cut into quarters.
3 Drain lamb from marinade; discard marinade. Char-grill (or grill or barbecue) lamb, until browned both sides and cooked as desired.
4 Serve lamb with beetroot; top with tzatziki.

lemon and olive lamb with couscous

LAMB AND MANGO SALAD WITH SWEET CHILLI DRESSING

on the table in **15 minutes** serves **4**
nutritional count per serving **10.8g total fat (3.1g
saturated fat); 1459kJ (349 cal); 26.2g carbohydrate;
33.9g protein; 5.1g fibre**

600g lamb fillets
1 tablespoon sesame oil
1 medium red onion (170g), sliced thinly
2 medium mangoes (860g), sliced
250g cherry tomatoes, halved
1 cup (80g) bean sprouts
1 cup chopped fresh coriander
sweet chilli dressing
¼ cup (60ml) sweet chilli sauce
1 tablespoon rice wine vinegar

1 Brush lamb with oil. Cook lamb on heated
oiled grill plate (or grill or barbecue) until
browned all over and cooked as desired.
2 Place onion, mango, tomato, sprouts and
coriander in large bowl.
3 Place ingredients for sweet chilli dressing in
screw-top jar; shake well.
4 Thinly slice lamb, add to salad with dressing;
toss gently to combine.

POTATO AND BACON FRITTATA

on the table in 35 minutes serves 4
nutritional count per serving 26g total fat (6.9g
saturated fat); 2136kJ (511 cal); 31.5g carbohydrate;
35.1g protein; 4.3g fibre

2 tablespoons olive oil
1 large brown onion (200g), halved,
**   sliced thinly**
5 bacon rashers (350g), chopped coarsely
2 teaspoons crushed garlic
1kg potatoes, peeled, chopped coarsely
6 eggs
2 tablespoons water

1 Heat half of the oil in frying pan (21cm base,
28cm top); cook onion, bacon and garlic,
stirring, until onion is soft. Add potato; cook,
stirring, about 10 minutes or until tender.
Transfer mixture to medium bowl.
2 Coat inside of same cleaned pan with
remaining oil; spread potato mixture in pan.
3 Whisk eggs and the water in medium bowl
until well combined; pour over potato mixture.
Cook frittata over low heat, covered loosely with
foil, about 8 minutes or until base is browned.
4 Place frittata under hot grill until it has set,
and top is browned.
serve with a mixed green salad.

PORK

pork with white bean puree

RED CURRY PORK WITH BASIL

on the table in 20 minutes serves 4
nutritional count per serving 21.5g total fat (9.8g
saturated fat); 1605kJ (384 cal); 6.8g carbohydrate;
39.5g protein; 3.2g fibre

1 medium red capsicum (200g)
1 medium green capsicum (200g)
1 medium yellow capsicum (200g)
8 thin pork steaks (650g)
2 tablespoons thai red curry paste
140ml can coconut cream
1 tablespoon peanut oil
¾ cup (180ml) chicken stock
¼ cup shredded fresh basil

1 Quarter capsicums, remove seeds and
membranes. Cook capsicum on heated oiled
grill plate (or grill or barbecue) until just tender.
2 Spread each pork steak with ½ teaspoon
curry paste and 2 teaspoons coconut cream.
Fold in half to seal.
3 Heat oil in large frying pan; cook pork until
browned on both sides and cooked through.
Remove from pan; cover to keep warm.
4 Add remaining paste to same pan; cook,
stirring, until fragrant. Add stock; bring to the
boil. Stir in remaining coconut cream and basil
until heated through. Serve pork with sauce
and capsicum.

serve with steamed rice.

PORK WITH WHITE BEAN PUREE

on the table in 20 minutes serves 4
nutritional count per serving 17.3g total fat (4.3g
saturated fat); 1634kJ (391 cal); 11.7g carbohydrate;
44.4g protein; 6g fibre

4 pork cutlets (1kg)
250g cherry tomatoes
2 tablespoons olive oil
2 x 300g cans white beans, rinsed, drained
2 teaspoons crushed garlic
1 tablespoon lemon juice

1 Brush pork and tomatoes with half of the oil;
cook pork and tomatoes on heated oiled grill
plate (or grill or barbecue) until pork is browned
on both sides and cooked through, and
tomatoes are soft.
2 Meanwhile, place beans in medium saucepan,
cover with water; bring to the boil. Reduce heat;
simmer, uncovered, until beans are heated
through. Drain well.
3 Blend or process beans with remaining oil,
garlic and juice until smooth.
4 Serve pork with tomatoes and bean puree.
serve with lemon wedges.

PORK WITH WHITE WINE SAUCE

on the table in **15 minutes** serves 4
nutritional count per serving **19.1g total fat (8.9g
saturated fat); 1476kJ (353 cal); 0.4g carbohydrate;
40g protein; 0.1g fibre**

**1 tablespoon olive oil
4 x 180g pork scotch fillet steaks
½ cup (125ml) dry white wine
½ cup (125ml) chicken stock
50g butter, chopped
2 tablespoons chopped fresh flat-leaf parsley**

1 Heat oil in large frying pan; cook pork, in
batches, until browned on both sides and just
cooked through. Remove from pan; cover to
keep warm.
2 Add wine to same pan, bring to the boil; add
stock and simmer, uncovered, until reduced by
a third. Stir in butter until melted; stir in parsley.
3 Cut pork into slices; serve with sauce.
serve with steamed baby new potatoes and sugar
snap peas.

pork and snake bean madras

PORK AND SNAKE BEAN MADRAS

on the table in **20 minutes** serves 4
nutritional count per serving **19.6g total fat (4.9g
saturated fat); 1802kJ (431 cal); 5.8g carbohydrate;
55.4g protein; 4.5g fibre**

**4 rindless bacon rashers (260g),
chopped coarsely
1 tablespoon peanut oil
700g pork fillets, sliced thinly
1 large white onion (200g), sliced thinly
¼ cup (65g) madras curry paste
200g snake beans, chopped coarsely
½ cup (125ml) beef stock
1 tablespoon tomato paste**

1 Stir-fry bacon in dry heated wok until crisp;
drain on absorbent paper.
2 Heat oil in same wok; stir-fry pork and onion,
in batches, until browned.
3 Stir-fry curry paste in same wok until just
fragrant. Add beans to wok with pork mixture,
bacon, stock and paste; stir-fry, tossing until
sauce boils.

PORK BUTTERFLY STEAKS WITH RADICCHIO

on the table in 15 minutes serves 4
nutritional count per serving 19.6g total fat (5.1g
saturated fat); 1626kJ (389 cal); 3.6g carbohydrate;
47.4g protein; 3.5g fibre

4 pork butterfly steaks (625g)
1 teaspoon fennel seeds, crushed
2 tablespoons olive oil
1 large radicchio (500g)
3 bacon rashers (210g), chopped
1 teaspoon crushed garlic
4 small egg tomatoes (240g), sliced thickly
1 tablespoon red wine vinegar
1 teaspoon brown sugar

1 Sprinkle both sides of pork steaks with fennel seeds.
2 Heat half of the oil in large frying pan; cook pork until browned on both sides and just cooked through. Remove from pan; cover to keep warm.
3 Meanwhile, cut radicchio into quarters, remove core, then cut each wedge in half.
4 Cook bacon in same pan, stirring, until browned and crisp. Add remaining oil, garlic, radicchio, tomato, vinegar and sugar to pan; cook, stirring, until lettuce is just wilted.
5 Serve pork with hot radicchio mixture.

pork and gai lan stir-fry

PORK AND GAI LAN STIR-FRY

on the table in 15 minutes serves 4
nutritional count per serving 18.3g total fat (4.8g saturated fat); 3093kJ (740 cal); 75.4g carbohydrate; 60.3g protein; 12.4g fibre

500g fresh singapore noodles
2 tablespoons peanut oil
750g pork strips
1 large brown onion (200g), sliced
1 teaspoon crushed garlic
1kg gai lan, chopped coarsely
⅓ cup (80ml) oyster sauce
1 tablespoon soy sauce

1 Place noodles in large heatproof bowl, cover with boiling water, stir gently to separate noodles; drain.
2 Heat half of the oil in wok; stir-fry pork, in batches, until browned and cooked through.
3 Heat remaining oil in wok; stir-fry onion and garlic until onion is soft. Return pork to wok with gai lan, combined sauces and noodles; stir-fry until gai lan is just wilted.

salami and vegetable pasta

SALAMI AND VEGETABLE PASTA

on the table in 20 minutes serves 4
nutritional count per serving 28.5g total fat (8.2g saturated fat); 2918kJ (698 cal); 80.7g carbohydrate; 26.3g protein; 7.5g fibre

375g spiral pasta
2 tablespoons olive oil
1 large brown onion (200g), chopped
1 large red capsicum (350g), chopped
3 finger eggplants (180g), sliced thickly
150g sliced salami
400g jar tomato pasta sauce
2 tablespoons chopped fresh flat-leaf parsley
½ cup (40g) flaked parmesan cheese

1 Cook pasta in large saucepan of boiling water until just tender; drain.
2 Meanwhile, heat oil in large frying pan; cook onion, capsicum, eggplant and salami, stirring, until vegetables are tender. Stir in sauce and parsley until hot.
3 Combine pasta and vegetable mixture; serve sprinkled with cheese.

LINGUINE WITH TUNA, LEMON AND ROCKET

on the table in 20 minutes serves 4
nutritional count per serving 35.4g total fat (5.3g
saturated fat); 3449kJ (825 cal); 86.5g carbohydrate;
37g protein; 4.8g fibre

425g can tuna in oil
500g linguine pasta
2 tablespoons extra virgin olive oil
2 teaspoons crushed garlic
2 dried medium red chillies, sliced thinly
⅓ cup (80ml) lemon juice
100g baby rocket leaves

1 Drain tuna over small bowl; reserve oil (you will
need ⅓ cup (80ml) oil).
2 Cook pasta in large saucepan of boiling water
until just tender; drain, return to pan.
3 Meanwhile, heat tuna oil and olive oil gently
in large frying pan, add garlic and chilli; cook,
stirring, until fragrant.
4 Add tuna to pan and break into chunks.
Remove from heat, then add juice.
5 Add tuna mixture to hot pasta with rocket;
toss gently to combine.

SEAFOOD

spaghetti with tomato and anchovy sauce

SALAD NICOISE

on the table in 20 minutes serves 4
nutritional count per serving 38.2g total fat (6.9g saturated fat); 2307kJ (552 cal); 17.2g carbohydrate; 32.7g protein; 5.2g fibre

200g baby green beans
2 baby cos lettuce
4 hard-boiled eggs, quartered
425g can tuna in brine, drained, flaked
½ medium red onion (85g), sliced
200g black olives
200g cherry tomatoes, halved
dill dressing
1 tablespoon wholegrain mustard
½ cup (125ml) olive oil
⅓ cup (80ml) lemon juice
1 teaspoon crushed garlic
1 tablespoon chopped fresh dill

1 Boil, steam or microwave beans until just tender; drain, rinse under cold water, drain.
2 Make dill dressing.
3 Arrange lettuce, beans, egg, tuna, onion, olives and tomato in serving bowls; drizzle with dressing.
dill dressing Place ingredients in screw-top jar; shake well.

SPAGHETTI WITH TOMATO AND ANCHOVY SAUCE

on the table in 25 minutes serves 4
nutritional count per serving 7.6g total fat (1.1g saturated fat); 2387kJ (571 cal); 98.9g carbohydrate; 21g protein; 8.8g fibre

500g spaghetti
1 tablespoon olive oil
2 medium red capsicums (400g), sliced thinly
2 medium yellow capsicums (400g), sliced thinly
5 green onions, sliced thinly
2 x 415g cans tomatoes
56g can anchovy fillets, drained, chopped finely
2 tablespoons chopped fresh chives
2 tablespoons chopped fresh flat-leaf parsley

1 Cook pasta in large saucepan of boiling water until just tender; drain.
2 Meanwhile, heat oil in large frying pan; cook capsicums, stirring, until soft.
3 Add onion, undrained crushed tomatoes, anchovy and herbs; bring to the boil. Reduce heat; simmer, uncovered, about 10 minutes or until thickened slightly. Serve sauce over pasta.

salad niçoise

salmon kedgeree

SALMON KEDGEREE

on the table in 20 minutes serves 4
nutritional count per serving 32.2g total fat (13g
saturated fat); 2111kJ (505 cal); 25.5g carbohydrate;
27.7g protein; 2.1g fibre

1 tablespoon olive oil
1 large brown onion (200g), sliced thinly
60g butter, chopped
1 teaspoon crushed garlic
2 teaspoons curry powder
4 green onions, sliced thinly
⅓ cup (40g) frozen peas
4 cups cooked white long-grain rice
415g can red salmon, drained
2 tablespoons chopped fresh flat-leaf parsley
1 tablespoon lemon juice
3 hard-boiled eggs, chopped coarsely

1 Heat oil in large frying pan; cook brown onion,
stirring, until browned. Remove from pan; cover
to keep warm.
2 Heat butter in same pan; cook garlic, curry
powder and green onion, stirring, until fragrant.
3 Add peas, rice and salmon, stir until heated
through. Stir in parsley and juice.
4 Serve kedgeree topped with egg and
brown onion.

note You will need to cook about 1⅓ cups (265g)
white long-grain rice for this recipe.

fish with wasabi mayonnaise

FISH WITH WASABI MAYONNAISE

on the table in 15 minutes serves 4
nutritional count per serving 17.6g total fat (3.4g
saturated fat); 1450kJ (347 cal); 5.8g carbohydrate;
41.2g protein; 0.3g fibre

1 tablespoon peanut oil
4 firm white fish fillets (800g)
⅓ cup (100g) mayonnaise
1-2 tablespoons wasabi paste, to taste
2 green onions, chopped finely
2 tablespoons chopped fresh coriander
2 tablespoons lime juice

1 Heat oil in large frying pan; cook fish until
browned on both sides and just cooked through.
2 Meanwhile, combine mayonnaise, wasabi,
onion, coriander and juice in small bowl.
3 Serve fish with wasabi mayonnaise.
serve with lemon wedges and steamed gai lan.

lemon ginger fish fillets

SWORDFISH WITH THAI DRESSING

on the table in 15 minutes serves 4
nutritional count per serving 5.1g total fat (1.5g saturated fat); 1007kJ (241 cal); 4.9g carbohydrate; 41.9g protein; 1.5g fibre

4 swordfish steaks (800g)
thai dressing
⅓ cup (80ml) sweet chilli sauce
½ cup (125ml) lime juice
1 tablespoon fish sauce
2 teaspoons finely chopped fresh lemon grass
2 tablespoons finely chopped fresh coriander
½ cup finely chopped fresh mint
1 teaspoon grated fresh ginger

1 Cook fish on heated oiled grill plate (or grill or barbecue) until browned both sides and cooked as desired.
2 Make thai dressing.
3 Serve fish drizzled with dressing.
thai dressing Place ingredients in screw-top jar; shake well.
serve with lemon wedges and a mixed leaf salad.

LEMON GINGER FISH FILLETS

on the table in 15 minutes serves 4
nutritional count per serving 20.8g total fat (12.2g saturated fat); 1480kJ (354 cal); 0.6g carbohydrate; 41.1g protein; 0.2g fibre

4 firm white fish fillets (800g)
80g butter
1 teaspoon finely grated lemon rind
2 tablespoons lemon juice
1 teaspoon grated fresh ginger
2 tablespoons finely chopped fresh parsley
3 green onions, sliced thinly

1 Cook fish in large heated oiled frying pan until browned lightly both sides and cooked through.
2 Meanwhile, melt butter in small saucepan, add rind, juice and ginger; cook 1 minute. Stir in parsley and onion.
3 Serve sauce over fish.
serve with lemon wedges.

swordfish with thai dressing

THAI RED CURRY FISH

on the table in **15 minutes** serves **4**
nutritional count per serving 30g total fat (20g
saturated fat); 1977kJ (473 cal); 6.5g carbohydrate;
42.4g protein; 5.1g fibre

¼ cup (65g) red curry paste
1⅔ cups (400ml) coconut milk
½ cup (125ml) water
250g green beans, halved
750g firm white fish fillets, sliced thickly
¼ cup finely chopped fresh coriander leaves

1 Cook paste in large, heated non-stick frying
pan, stirring, until fragrant.
2 Add coconut milk and the water to pan;
bring to the boil. Add beans; simmer, covered,
2 minutes.
3 Add fish to pan; simmer, covered, until fish is
just cooked. Stir in coriander.
serve with steamed rice and lime wedges.

ZUCCHINI AND MUSHROOM OMELETTE

on the table in 15 minutes serves 1
nutritional count per serving 30.6g total fat (15.5g
saturated fat); 1597kJ (382 cal); 2.1g carbohydrate;
24.5g protein; 2g fibre

10g butter
1 teaspoon crushed garlic
25g button mushrooms, sliced thinly
¼ cup (50g) grated zucchini
1 green onion, chopped finely
2 eggs
1 tablespoon water
¼ cup (30g) grated cheddar cheese

1 Heat half of the butter in small frying pan,
add garlic and mushrooms; cook, stirring,
until mushrooms are just browned.
2 Add zucchini and onion to pan; cook, stirring,
until zucchini begins to soften. Remove mixture
from pan; cover to keep warm.
3 Whisk eggs and the water together in small
bowl; whisk in cheese until until combined.
4 Heat remaining butter in same pan, pour egg
mixture into pan; cook, tilting pan, over medium
heat until almost set.
5 Place vegetable mixture evenly over half of
the omelette; using eggslice, flip other half over
vegetable mixture. Using eggslice, slide omelette
gently onto serving plate.

fettuccine with cauliflower and broccoli

MOROCCAN CHICKPEA SOUP

on the table in 25 minutes serves 4
nutritional count per serving 8.7g total fat (1.7g
saturated fat); 1037kJ (248 cal); 25.8g carbohydrate;
12.9g protein; 8.1g fibre

1 tablespoon olive oil
1 large brown onion (200g), chopped finely
2 teaspoons crushed garlic
1 tablespoon grated ginger
1½ teaspoons ground cumin
1½ teaspoons ground coriander
1 teaspoon ground turmeric
½ teaspoon sweet paprika
¼ teaspoon ground cinnamon
1.5 litres (6 cups) vegetable stock
2 x 300g cans chickpeas, rinsed, drained
2 x 415g cans tomatoes
1 teaspoon grated lemon rind
1 tablespoon chopped fresh coriander

1 Heat oil in large saucepan; cook onion,
garlic and ginger, stirring, until onion is soft.
Add spices; cook, stirring, until fragrant.
2 Stir in stock, chickpeas and undrained
crushed tomatoes; bring to the boil. Reduce
heat; simmer, uncovered, 15 minutes or until
soup thickens slightly.
3 Just before serving, stir in rind and coriander.

moroccan chickpea soup

FETTUCCINE WITH CAULIFLOWER AND BROCCOLI

on the table in 30 minutes serves 4
nutritional count per serving 18.1g total fat (11.1g
saturated fat); 1843kJ (441 cal); 52.2g carbohydrate;
13.9g protein; 6.2g fibre

250g fettuccine
4 cups (350g) coarsely chopped cauliflower
4 cups (350g) coarsely chopped broccoli
80g butter
3 teaspoons crushed garlic
½ cup (35g) stale breadcrumbs

1 Cook pasta in large saucepan of boiling water
until just tender; drain.
2 Meanwhile, bring large saucepan of water to
the boil. Add cauliflower and broccoli; cook until
just tender, drain. Rinse under cold water, drain.
3 Heat butter in large frying pan, add garlic and
breadcrumbs; cook, stirring, until breadcrumbs
are golden brown.
4 Combine pasta in large bowl with cauliflower,
broccoli and breadcrumb mixture.
note You need half a medium cauliflower and about
450g broccoli for this recipe.

MUSHROOM PIZZA

on the table in 25 minutes serves 4

Sprinkle ¾ cup grated pizza cheese over four
112g pizza bases, then place on oven tray.
Divide 150g thinly sliced flat mushrooms,
100g crumbled fetta cheese and 2 tablespoons
chopped fresh chives among bases. Top
pizzas with another ¾ cup grated pizza cheese.
Bake pizzas at 220°C/200°C fan-forced for
15 minutes or until pizza tops are browned
lightly and bases are crisp.

KUMARA, ROSEMARY AND CARAMELISED ONION PIZZA

on the table in 35 minutes serves 4

Combine 2 tablespoons olive oil, 1 large coarsely
chopped kumara, 2 crushed cloves garlic,
1 tablespoon finely chopped rosemary and
1 teaspoon chilli flakes in medium shallow
baking dish; roast at 220°C/200°C fan-forced
about 20 minutes or until kumara is tender.
Meanwhile, melt 40g butter in medium frying
pan; cook 1 large thinly sliced red onion, stirring
occasionally, 15 minutes or until caramelised.
Place 4 large pitta breads on oven trays; spread
with 1 cup bottled tomato pasta sauce. Divide
kumara and onion among pitta; sprinkle with
2 cups coarsely grated mozzarella cheese.
Bake pizzas about 10 minutes or until pitta
bases are crisp and topping is heated through;
serve sprinkled with ½ cup fresh mint leaves.

SPINACH, CAPSICUM AND FETTA PIZZAS

on the table in **15 minutes** serves **4**

Spread ½ cup bottled tomato pasta sauce on 4 large pitta breads, then place on oven trays. Sprinkle pitta with 1 cup pizza cheese; top with 75g baby spinach leaves, 1 medium thinly sliced red capsicum and 100g crumbled fetta cheese; sprinkle with another 1 cup pizza cheese. Bake pizzas at 240°C/220°C fan-forced about 10 minutes or until browned.

PUMPKIN AND FETTA PIZZA

on the table in **25 minutes** serves **1**

Combine 50g piece pumpkin sliced into strips with a vegetable peeler and 1 teaspoon olive oil in small bowl. Spread 1 pocket pitta bread with 2 tablespoons bottled tomato pasta sauce; top with pumpkin and 25g crumbled reduced-fat fetta cheese. Bake pizza at 180°C/160°C fan-forced about 15 minutes or until pumpkin is tender. Serve sprinkled with 2 teaspoons finely chopped fresh mint leaves.

BURGHUL AND FETTA SALAD

on the table in 15 minutes serves 4
nutritional count per serving 12.5g total fat (7.7g saturated fat); 1216kJ (291 cal); 25.8g carbohydrate; 14.2g protein; 7.7g fibre

1½ cups (240g) burghul
200g green beans
⅓ cup (80ml) oil-free french dressing
2 tablespoons lemon juice
1½ cups firmly packed fresh flat-leaf parsley
½ cup chopped fresh mint
4 green onions, sliced
250g cherry tomatoes, halved
200g fetta cheese, crumbled

1 Place burghul in large bowl; cover with boiling water, set aside about 10 minutes or until burghul is just tender, drain. Pat dry with absorbent paper.
2 Meanwhile, cut beans into thirds; boil, steam or microwave until just tender. Drain.
3 Place burghul and beans in large bowl with dressing and remaining ingredients; toss gently to combine.

fresh tomato and chilli pasta

FRESH TOMATO AND CHILLI PASTA

on the table in 15 minutes serves 4
nutritional count per serving 23.2g total fat (4.9g saturated fat); 2792kJ (668 cal); 89.8g carbohydrate; 20.2g protein; 7.6g fibre

500g penne pasta
⅓ cup (80ml) olive oil
2 teaspoons crushed garlic
2 teaspoons chopped chilli
4 medium ripe tomatoes (800g), chopped
1 cup chopped fresh flat-leaf parsley
½ cup (40g) flaked parmesan cheese

1 Cook pasta in large saucepan of boiling water until just tender; drain.
2 Meanwhile, heat oil in large frying pan; cook garlic and chilli, stirring, about 1 minute or until fragrant. Stir in tomato and parsley; remove pan from heat.
3 Add sauce mixture to pasta; toss gently to combine. Serve topped with cheese.

burghul and fetta salad

ricotta ravioli with pumpkin sauce

RICOTTA RAVIOLI WITH PUMPKIN SAUCE

on the table in 30 minutes serves 4
nutritional count per serving 33.8g total fat (9.5g
saturated fat); 2107kJ (504 cal); 34.6g carbohydrate;
13.9g protein; 5.1g fibre

¼ cup (60ml) olive oil
1 small brown onion (80g), chopped finely
1 clove garlic, crushed
600g butternut pumpkin, sliced thinly
1½ cups (375ml) vegetable stock
½ teaspoon ground nutmeg
½ cup (125ml) thickened light cream
600g fresh ricotta ravioli
⅓ cup (50g) pine nuts, roasted
2 tablespoons coarsely chopped fresh chives

1 Heat half of the oil in large frying pan; cook
onion and garlic, stirring, until onion is soft.
Remove from pan.
2 Heat remaining oil in same pan; cook pumpkin
until browned both sides. Return onion to pan
with stock and nutmeg; cook, stirring, until liquid
is absorbed and pumpkin mashed. Stir in cream.
3 Meanwhile, cook pasta in large saucepan of
boiling water until tender; drain.
4 Serve pasta with pumpkin sauce, top with
pine nuts and chives.

mixed mushrooms in garlic butter

MIXED MUSHROOMS IN GARLIC BUTTER

on the table in 25 minutes serves 4
nutritional count per serving 30.6g total fat (15.2g
saturated fat); 1522kJ (364 cal); 7.5g carbohydrate;
11.7g protein; 8.4g fibre

400g flat mushrooms
2 tablespoons peanut oil
1 large brown onion (200g), sliced thinly
2 cloves garlic, crushed
400g swiss brown mushrooms
400g button mushrooms
2 teaspoons garlic salt
100g butter

1 Quarter flat mushrooms. Heat oil in wok;
stir-fry onion, garlic and all mushrooms, in
batches, until tender.
2 Return mushrooms to wok with garlic salt and
chopped butter; stir-fry until butter is melted.
serve with toast, sprinkled with baby basil leaves.

Marino Branch
Brainse Marglann Mhuirine
Tel: 8336297

COCONUT PINEAPPLE

Peel, core and thinly slice fresh pineapple; divide among serving plates. Drizzle with passionfruit pulp, Malibu and toasted flaked coconut.

ICE-CREAM TOPPED MERINGUES

Place a scoop of boysenberry ripple ice-cream into meringue shells; drizzle with lemon curd.

PEACH CRUMBLES

Combine canned, drained peach slices with a little vanilla extract and ground cinnamon in individual serving dishes; top with crushed choc-chip cookies, a little butter and brown sugar. Bake at 180°C/160°C fan-forced until sugar melts and fruit is heated through.

BANANA AND PEANUT BRITTLE

Layer mascarpone, sliced bananas and crushed peanut brittle in a parfait glass.

RICOTTA AND BERRY BRIOCHE

Drizzle fresh ricotta with maple syrup; serve with mixed berries and toasted brioche.

PEAR TARTS

Place canned, drained pear halves on pieces of puff pastry; roll in edges of pastry to meet pears, sprinkle with brown sugar. Bake at 240°C/220°C fan-forced until pastry is puffed and golden.

CHOCOLATE FONDUE

Stir chopped chocolate, marshmallows and cream in saucepan over low heat until melted. Serve fondue with fresh fruit.

ICE-CREAM AFFOGATO

Top vanilla ice-cream with plunger coffee and Irish cream liqueur; serve with chocolate wafers.

BACON also called bacon slices.

BEAN SPROUTS also called bean shoots; tender new growths of beans and seeds germinated for consumption as sprouts.

BEANS

snake long (about 40cm), thin, round, fresh green beans, Asian in origin, with a taste similar to green or french beans. Used most frequently in stir-fries, they are also known as yard-long beans because of their (pre-metric) length.

white a generic term we use for canned or dried cannellini, haricot, navy or great northern beans belonging to the same family, *phaseolus vulgaris*.

BEEF, EYE FILLET STEAKS also known as beef tenderloin or fillet.

BEETROOT also known as red beets; firm, round root vegetable.

BLACK BEAN SAUCE a Chinese sauce made from fermented soy beans, spices, water and wheat flour.

BREADCRUMBS

packaged prepared fine-textured but crunchy white breadcrumbs; good for coating or crumbing foods that are to be fried

stale one- or two-day-old bread made into crumbs by grating, blending or processing.

BROCCOLINI a cross between broccoli and chinese kale; long asparagus-like stems with a long loose floret, both completely edible. Resembles broccoli but is milder and sweeter in taste.

BURGHUL also called bulghur wheat; hulled steamed wheat kernels that, once dried, are crushed into various sized grains. Used in Middle Eastern dishes. Is not the same as cracked wheat.

BUTTER we use salted or unsalted (sweet) butter; 125g is equal to one stick of butter.

CAPSICUM also known as bell pepper. Seeds and membranes should be discarded before use; available in several colours, each of which has an individual flavour.

CAYENNE PEPPER a thin-fleshed, long, extremely hot red chilli; usually purchased dried and ground.

CHEESE

cheddar a semi-hard cow-milk cheese. It ranges in colour from white to pale- yellow and has a slightly crumbly texture if properly matured. It's aged for between nine months and two years and the flavour becomes sharper with time.

fetta Greek in origin; a crumbly goat- or sheep-milk cheese having a sharp, salty taste. Ripened and stored in salted whey; particularly good cubed and tossed into salads.

parmesan also called parmigiano; is a hard, grainy cow-milk cheese originating in the Parma region of Italy. The curd for this cheese is salted in brine for a month, then aged for up to 2 years in humid conditions. Reggiano is the best parmesan, aged for a minimum 2 years and made only in the Italian region of Emilia-Romagna.

pizza a commercial blend of varying proportions of processed grated mozzarella, cheddar and parmesan.

CHICKEN

breast fillet skinned, boned chicken breast.

tenderloins thin strip of meat lying just under the breast.

thigh fillets skinned and boned thigh.

CHICKPEAS also called garbanzos, hummus or channa; an irregularly round, sandy-coloured legume used in Mediterranean and Latin cooking.

CHILLI

dried flakes dehydrated extremely fine slices and whole seeds; good for cooking or for sprinkling over cooked food.

red thai small hot bright-red chilli.

CHORIZO SAUSAGE Spanish in origin, made of coarsely ground pork and highly seasoned with garlic and chilli.

CIABATTA in Italian, the word means slipper, the traditional shape of this popular crisp-crusted, open-textured white sourdough bread. A good bread to use for bruschetta.

CINNAMON available both in the piece (called sticks or quills) and ground into powder; one of the world's most common spices, used universally as a sweet, fragrant flavouring for both sweet and savoury foods. The dried inner bark of the shoots of the Sri Lankan native cinnamon tree; much of what is sold as the real thing is in fact cassia, Chinese cinnamon, from the bark of the cassia tree. Less expensive to process than true cinnamon, it is often blended with Sri Lankan cinnamon to produce the type of "cinnamon" most commonly found in supermarkets.

COCONUT

cream obtained from the first pressing of the coconut flesh alone, without added water; available in cans and cartons.

milk not the liquid inside (coconut water), but the diluted liquid from the second pressing of grated coconut flesh; available in cans and cartons.

GLOSSARY

CORNFLOUR also known as cornstarch. Available made from corn or wheat (wheaten cornflour, gluten-free, gives a lighter texture in cakes); used as a thickening agent in cooking.

COS LETTUCE also known as romaine lettuce; the traditional caesar salad lettuce. Long, with leaves ranging from dark green on the outside to almost white near the core; the leaves have a stiff centre rib giving a slight cupping effect to the leaf on either side.

COUSCOUS a fine, grain-like cereal product, originally from North Africa; made from semolina. It is rehydrated by steaming or with the addition of a warm liquid and swells to three or four times its original size.

CUMIN also known as zeera.

CURRY PASTES commercial curry pastes vary in their heat intensity so, while we specify a measurement in our recipes, you might try using less of the paste you've purchased until you can determine how hot it makes the final dish.

CURRY POWDER a blend of ground spices, often including dried chilli, cinnamon, coriander, cumin, fennel, fenugreek, mace, cardamom and turmeric. Available mild or hot.

EGGPLANT also called aubergine.

EGGS some recipes in this book may call for raw or barely cooked eggs; exercise caution if there is a salmonella problem in your area.

FISH SAUCE called nam pla on the label if it is Thai made; the Vietnamese version, nuoc nam, is almost identical. Made from pulverised salted fermented fish (most often anchovies); has a pungent smell and strong taste.

GAI LAN also known as chinese broccoli and chinese kale; green vegetable appreciated more for its stems than its coarse leaves. Can be served steamed and stir-fried, in soups and noodle dishes. One of the most popular Asian greens.

GINGER, FRESH also called green or root ginger; the thick gnarled root of a tropical plant. Can be kept, peeled, covered with dry sherry in a jar and refrigerated, or frozen in an airtight container.

KAFFIR LIME LEAVES also known as bai magrood and looks like two glossy dark green leaves joined end to end, forming a rounded hourglass shape. Sold fresh, dried or frozen, the dried leaves are less potent so double the number if using them as a substitute for fresh; a strip of fresh lime peel may be substituted for each kaffir lime leaf.

KECAP MANIS a dark, thick sweet soy sauce used in most South-East Asian cuisines. Depending on the manufacturer, its sweetness is derived from the addition of palm sugar or molasses when brewed.

LEBANESE CUCUMBERS long, slender and thin-skinned; this variety also known as the european or burpless cucumber.

LEMON GRASS also called takrai, serai or serah. A tall, clumping, lemon-smelling and tasting, sharp-edged aromatic tropical grass; the white lower part of the stem is used, finely chopped. Can be found, fresh, dried, powdered and frozen, in supermarkets, greengrocers and Asian food shops.

LEMON PEPPER SEASONING a blend of crushed black pepper, lemon, herbs and spices.

LENTILS (red, brown, yellow) dried pulses often identified by and named after their colour.

MARSALA a sweet fortified wine, originally from Sicily.

MESCLUN pronounced mess-kluhn; also known as mixed greens or spring salad mix. A commercial blend of assorted young lettuce and other green leaves, including baby spinach leaves, mizuna and curly endive.

MUSHROOMS

button small, cultivated white mushrooms with a mild flavour. When we call for an unspecified type of mushroom, use button.

flat large and flat with a rich earthy flavour. They are sometimes misnamed field mushrooms which are wild mushrooms.

swiss brown also known as roman or cremini. Light to dark brown mushrooms with full-bodied flavour; suited for use in casseroles or being stuffed and baked.

MUSTARD, WHOLEGRAIN also known as seeded. A French-style coarse-grain mustard made from crushed mustard seeds and dijon-style French mustard.

NOODLES

dried rice dried noodles made from rice flour and water, available flat and wide or very thin (vermicelli). Should be soaked in boiling water to soften. Also called rice stick noodles.

fried crispy egg noodles that have been deep-fried then packaged for sale on supermarket shelves.

hokkien also known as stir-fry noodles; fresh wheat noodles resembling thick, yellow-brown spaghetti needing no pre-cooking before use.

singapore pre-cooked wheat noodles best described as a thinner version of hokkien; sold, packaged, in the refrigerated section of supermarkets.

NUTMEG a strong and pungent spice ground from the dried nut of an evergreen tree native to Indonesia. Usually found ground but the flavour is more intense from a whole nut, available from spice shops, so it's best to grate your own. Used most often in baking and milk-based desserts, but also works nicely in savoury dishes. Found in mixed spice mixtures.

OIL

olive made from ripened olives. Extra virgin and virgin are the best while extra light or light refers to taste not fat levels.

peanut pressed from ground peanuts; most commonly used oil in Asian cooking because of its high smoke point (capacity to handle high heat without burning).

sesame made from toasted, crushed, white sesame seeds; used as a flavouring rather than a cooking medium.

vegetable any of a number of oils sourced from plant rather than animal fats.

ONION

green also known as scallion or (incorrectly) shallot; an immature onion picked before the bulb has formed, having a long, bright-green edible stalk.

red also known as spanish, red spanish or bermuda onion; a sweet-flavoured, large, purple-red onion.

spring have crisp, narrow, green-leafed tops and a large, sweet white bulb.

OYSTER SAUCE Asian in origin, this rich, brown sauce is made from oysters and their brine, salt and soy sauce, and thickened with starches.

PAPRIKA ground dried red capsicum (bell pepper), available sweet or hot.

PINE NUTS also called pignoli; not a nut but a small, cream-coloured kernel from pine cones. They are best roasted before use to bring out the flavour.

POTATOES

baby new also known as chats; not a separate variety but an early harvest with very thin skin. Good unpeeled steamed, eaten hot or cold in salads.

coliban round, smooth white skin and flesh; good for baking and mashing.

desiree oval, smooth and pink-skinned, waxy yellow flesh; good in salads, boiled and roasted.

PROSCIUTTO a kind of unsmoked Italian ham; salted, air-cured and aged, it is usually eaten uncooked.

RADICCHIO Italian in origin; a member of the chicory family. The dark burgundy leaves and strong, bitter flavour can be cooked or eaten raw in salads.

ROCKET also known as arugula, rugula and rucola; a peppery-tasting green leaf which can be eaten raw in salad or used in cooking.

SAMBAL OELEK (also ulek or olek) Indonesian salty paste made from ground chillies and vinegar.

SNOW PEAS also called mange tout ("eat all"). Snow pea tendrils, the growing shoots of the plant, are sold by greengrocers.

SOY SAUCE also known as sieu; made from fermented soybeans.

Several variations are available in supermarkets and Asian food stores; we use japanese soy sauce unless indicated otherwise.

SPINACH also known as english spinach and, incorrectly, silverbeet. Tender green leaves are good raw in salads or added to soups, stir-fries and stews.

SUGAR

brown an extremely soft, fine granulated sugar retaining molasses for its characteristic colour and flavour.

caster also known as superfine or finely granulated table sugar.

VINEGAR

balsamic Authentic only from the province of Modena, Italy; made from a regional wine of white Trebbiano grapes aged in antique wooden casks to give the exquisite pungent flavour.

rice a colourless vinegar made from fermented rice and flavoured with sugar and salt. Also known as seasoned rice vinegar; sherry can be substituted.

WASABI also called wasabe; an Asian horseradish used to make the pungent, green-coloured sauce traditionally served with Japanese raw fish dishes; sold in powdered or paste form.

WOMBOK also known as Chinese cabbage, peking or napa cabbage; elongated in shape with pale green, crinkly leaves, this is the most common cabbage in South-East Asia. Can be shredded or chopped and eaten raw or braised, steamed or stir-fried.

YOGURT we used plain, unflavoured yogurt, unless otherwise specified.

ZUCCHINI also known as courgette.

CONVERSION CHART

MEASURES

One Australian metric measuring cup holds approximately 250ml, one Australian metric tablespoon holds 20ml, one Australian metric teaspoon holds 5ml.

The difference between one country's measuring cups and another's is within a 2- or 3-teaspoon variance, and will not affect your cooking results. North America, New Zealand and the United Kingdom use a 15ml tablespoon. All cup and spoon measurements are level. The most accurate way of measuring dry ingredients is to weigh them. When measuring liquids, use a clear glass or plastic jug with metric markings.

We use large eggs with an average weight of 60g.

DRY MEASURES

METRIC	IMPERIAL
15g	½oz
30g	1oz
60g	2oz
90g	3oz
125g	4oz (¼lb)
155g	5oz
185g	6oz
220g	7oz
250g	8oz (½lb)
280g	9oz
315g	10oz
345g	11oz
375g	12oz (¾lb)
410g	13oz
440g	14oz
470g	15oz
500g	16oz (1lb)
750g	24oz (1½lb)
1kg	32oz (2lb)

LIQUID MEASURES

METRIC	IMPERIAL
30ml	1 fluid oz
60ml	2 fluid oz
100ml	3 fluid oz
125ml	4 fluid oz
150ml	5 fluid oz (¼ pint/1 gill)
190ml	6 fluid oz
250ml	8 fluid oz
300ml	10 fluid oz (½ pint)
500ml	16 fluid oz
600ml	20 fluid oz (1 pint)
1000ml (1 litre)	1¾ pints

LENGTH MEASURES

METRIC	IMPERIAL
3mm	⅛in
6mm	¼in
1cm	½in
2cm	¾in
2.5cm	1in
5cm	2in
6cm	2½in
8cm	3in
10cm	4in
13cm	5in
15cm	6in
18cm	7in
20cm	8in
23cm	9in
25cm	10in
28cm	11in
30cm	12in (1ft)

OVEN TEMPERATURES

These oven temperatures are only a guide for conventional ovens.
For fan-forced ovens, check the manufacturer's manual.

	°C (CELSIUS)	°F (FAHRENHEIT)	GAS MARK
Very slow	120	250	½
Slow	150	275-300	1-2
Moderately slow	160	325	3
Moderate	180	350-375	4-5
Moderately hot	200	400	6
Hot	220	425-450	7-8
Very hot	240	475	9

INDEX

If you like this cookbook, you'll love these...

These are just a small selection of titles available in *The Australian Women's Weekly* range
on sale at selected newsagents and supermarkets or online at www.acpbooks.com.au